W9-BYZ-293

JANE GOODALL

Revolutionary Primatologist and Anthropologist

by Lois Sepahban

Content Consultant
Kevin D. Hunt
Professor of Anthropology and Animal Behavior
Indiana University Bloomington

Core Library

An Imprint of Abdo Publishing
abdopublishing.com

abdopublishing.com

Published by Abdo Publishing, a division of ABDO, PO Box 398166, Minneapolis, Minnesota 55439. Copyright © 2016 by Abdo Consulting Group, Inc. International copyrights reserved in all countries. No part of this book may be reproduced in any form without written permission from the publisher. Core Library™ is a trademark and logo of Abdo Publishing.

Printed in the United States of America, North Mankato, Minnesota
022015
092015

Cover Photo: Peter Kramer/Getty Images
Interior Photos: Peter Kramer/Getty Images, 1; Stephen Robinson/NHPA/Photoshot/Newscom, 4; AP Images, 8; Edgar Rice Burroughs, 10; Gerry Ellis/Minden Pictures/Newscom, 12; Everett Collection/Newscom, 17, 28, 45; Morphart Creation/Shutterstock Images, 18; Bettmann/Corbis, 20; Ingo Arndt/Minden Pictures/Corbis, 24, 43; Erik Hersman, 30; Red Line Editorial, 33; David Higgs/NHPA/Photoshot/Newscom, 34; Stefan Rousseau/EPA/Newscom, 36; Bela Szandelszky/AP Images, 40

Editor: Jenna Gleisner
Series Designer: Becky Daum

Library of Congress Control Number: 2015931131

Cataloging-in-Publication Data
Sepahban, Lois.
 Jane Goodall: Revolutionary primatologist and anthropologist / Lois Sepahban.
   p. cm. -- (Great minds of science)
Includes bibliographical references and index.
ISBN 978-1-62403-875-4
1. Goodall, Jane, 1934- --Juvenile literature. 2. Primatologists--England--Biography--Juvenile literature. 3. Women primatologists--Biography--Juvenile literature.   I. Title.
590.92--dc23
[B]   2015931131

CONTENTS

CHAPTER ONE

AN EARLY OBSERVER

O n April 3, 1934, Jane Goodall was born Valerie Jane Morris-Goodall in London, England. She was the first child of Mortimer and Vanne Goodall. While growing up, Jane did not have a television, video games, or even a bicycle. But Jane's family did have a little garden, and she loved spending time in it. She watched the dogs,

Jane Goodall grew up to become one of the most influential primatologists of all time.

cats, and birds that visited the park near her house. She collected insects and worms.

At age four, Jane already had the mind of a scientist. She wanted to learn about animals, so she observed them. She watched and learned. Then she shared her new knowledge with anyone who would listen. Often, that was her mother. Jane's mother encouraged her to explore and learn more about animals.

The Henhouse

When she was four years old, Jane and her family stayed with her grandmother on her grandmother's family farm. While there, Jane became curious about the hens. She knew that eggs came from chickens, but she didn't know how. Jane hid in the henhouse so she wouldn't scare the hens. Then she waited. She waited for nearly four hours but was finally rewarded. A hen entered the henhouse and laid an egg right in front of her.

Europe at War

In 1939, when Jane was five years old, her world changed as countries around the world entered World War II (1939–1945). Germany, led by Adolf Hitler, began invading other countries in Europe.

Jane's father joined the British Army. Jane, her mother, and Jane's sister moved to a new home in Bournemouth. Jane's two aunts also lived with them.

Warfare destroyed cities and left many people homeless. Two homeless women came to live with Jane and her family. With many people living in their home, Jane learned that everyone had to work together, no matter their differences.

Jane had a loving family and a happy home, but she could never forget the terrible suffering caused by the war. News reports of war made Jane think about how people

The Birches

After her father joined the military to fight in World War II, Jane, her mother, and her sister moved to the Birches. The Birches is the name of the house Jane's mother grew up in. It is located in Bournemouth, a village in southwest England, right on the English Channel. Living at the Birches allowed Jane's love for nature and animals to grow. Today the Birches is still a family home. Jane's sister lives there, and so does Jane when she is not traveling around the world.

During World War II, German forces bombed London and other cities.

could be cruel. Hitler's cruelty led him to imprison and kill 6 million Jewish people during the war. This mass killing became known as the Holocaust.

When the war ended in 1945, Jane was 11 years old. She was grateful that her father returned home from the war when so many other men did not. But she began to ask new questions. She wondered how people could behave in such cruel ways.

The Animal Lover

Jane found comfort observing and spending time with the animals at the house in Bournemouth. She had many pets, including cats, birds, guinea pigs, and tortoises. Her favorite pet was a dog named Rusty. Rusty followed Jane as she explored the natural world around her.

When she wanted to be alone, Jane read stories about animals. Her favorite books were *The Wind in the Willows*, *The Story of Doctor Dolittle*, and *The Jungle Book*. She also loved reading Edgar Rice Burroughs's Tarzan books. In those books, baby Tarzan is adopted by a family of apes after his human parents die. While reading about Tarzan, Jane imagined living in Africa with animal friends, especially apes, just like Tarzan. When she told her mother about her dreams, her mother encouraged her. Jane's mother told her that if she worked hard, she could make her dream come true.

Edgar Rice Burroughs's Tarzan books inspired film adaptations.

Jane was a good student and earned good enough grades to go to college. Jane wanted to have a career working with animals. Unfortunately her family did not have enough money to send her to college. But Jane wasn't ready to give up.

In Jane Goodall's autobiography, *Reason for Hope: A Spiritual Journey*, she reveals how World War II changed her thoughts about humanity:

> *By the time I was seven I was used to news of battles, of defeats and of victories. Knowledge of man's inhumanity to man became more real as the newspapers and radio hinted at unspeakable horrors perpetrated on the Jews of Europe and the cruelties of [Hitler]. Although my own life was still filled with love and security I was slowly becoming aware of another kind of world altogether, a harsh and bitter world of pain and death and human cruelty. And although we were among the luckiest, far away from the horror of massive bombings, nevertheless, signs of war were all around.*

> *Source: Jane Goodall. Reason for Hope: A Spiritual Journey. New York: Warner Books, 1999. Print. 112–113.*

What's the Big Idea?

Take a close look at this passage. What is Jane trying to say about how cruel people can be to each other? Pick out two details she uses to make her point.

CHAPTER TWO

OBSERVING IN AFRICA

By the time Goodall graduated from high school in 1952, she had two goals. She wanted to go to Africa, and she wanted to work with animals. Because her family didn't have enough money to pay for a college education, Goodall's mother encouraged her to begin working as a secretary.

Goodall's dream of visiting Africa came true in 1957.

In 1956, when Goodall was 22 years old, she received a letter from her friend and former classmate, Marie Claude "Clo" Mange. After the war, Clo's father had bought a farm in Kenya, a country in eastern Africa. Goodall was determined to find a way to visit. Goodall was living away from home and working as a secretary at the time. She decided to move back home so that she could save every penny she earned. She got a job as a waitress and worked as many hours as she could. It took Goodall five months to save up enough money for the trip to Africa. In 1957 she traveled by ship and train from London to Nairobi, the capital of Kenya, where her friend met her.

Goodall Finds a Mentor

After spending a few weeks at Clo's farm, Goodall moved to Nairobi and found a job as a secretary. She quickly made new friends. When Goodall told her friends that she wanted to work with animals, they suggested she meet Louis Leakey, who studied prehistoric humans and was involved with field studies of apes in Africa.

With this advice in mind, Goodall called Leakey and asked him if he would meet with her. Within two months, they met. Based on their conversation, Leakey saw that Goodall was intelligent. He admired her interest in learning about animals. He needed help with his studies, so he offered Goodall a job as his secretary. While she worked for Leakey, Goodall joined his family on an archaeological dig. The dig took place at Olduvai Gorge in Tanganyika, or present-day Tanzania. The team stayed there for three months and camped in tents. At night Goodall was

Goodall's Pets

While living in Nairobi, Goodall found many animals to love. Her first pets were a fox she named Chimba and a monkey she named Levi. Goodall was devastated when a group of street thugs killed Chimba. She bought a mongoose named Kip and another monkey named Kombo to keep Levi company. Goodall's family of pets kept growing.

excited and also a little bit frightened to hear hyenas, lions, wildebeests, and zebras not far from their tents. During that time, Leakey talked to Goodall about apes, such as chimpanzees, gorillas, and bonobos. He told her that he wanted to learn about their behavior because he thought it would teach him about the behavior of the prehistoric humans he was studying. He needed someone who would go out into the bush, or the wilderness where wild animals lived, to study chimpanzees. Leakey thought Goodall would be the perfect fit. He didn't want a scientist who was

Olduvai Gorge

Olduvai Gorge is located in the northern part of modern-day Tanzania. Beginning in the 1930s, Leakey took teams to Olduvai Gorge to search for fossils. He was particularly interested in early human fossils. He also discovered the fossilized remains of other animals and plants. Olduvai Gorge is a unique location because the fossils found there show several important moments in human evolution, or the development of modern humans. It is the first place early stone tools were discovered.

trained to look at nature in a certain way. He thought
Goodall would be more open to new ways of looking
at nature. But there was one problem.

Gaining Permission

It was 1958, and government officials thought it was
too dangerous for a young, single woman to live alone

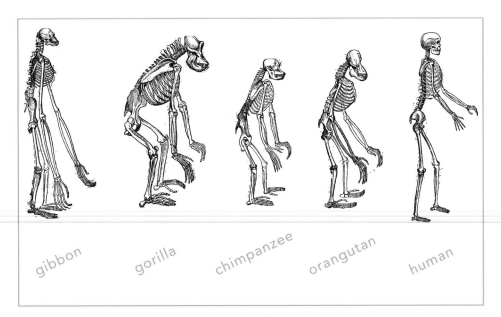

Comparing Human and Ape Skeletons
This diagram shows the skeletal similarities between
gibbons, gorillas, chimpanzees, orangutans, and humans.
What similarities do you notice about each of the skeletons?
What differences do you notice? How does seeing this
diagram help you better understand why scientists such as
Leakey and Goodall wanted to study chimpanzees?

in the bush to study animals. The British government
wouldn't give Goodall permission unless she had a
companion to go with her. Leakey wrote to Goodall's
mother to explain the situation, and Goodall's mother
traveled to Africa to solve the problem. Goodall's
mother once again encouraged Goodall's dreams by
living with her so she could study chimpanzees.

In 1960, at the age of 26, Goodall heard the good news she had been hoping for. The government gave her permission to study chimpanzees in the bush as long as her mother stayed with her. Leakey found the perfect place for Goodall's research to take place: Gombe, in Tanganyika. Goodall's dreams were beginning to come true. She was in Africa, and she was on her way to the bush to live among wild chimpanzees.

EXPLORE ONLINE

The website below has information about Goodall's work with chimpanzees as well as more information about chimpanzees. As you know, every source is different. Reread Chapter Two of this book. What are the similarities between Chapter Two and the information you found on the website? Are there any differences? How do the two sources present information differently?

The Jane Goodall Institute: Chimpanzees
mycorelibrary.com/jane-goodall

CHAPTER THREE

GETTING TO KNOW CHIMPANZEES

Goodall and her mother arrived at the Gombe Stream Chimpanzee Reserve, a 20-square-mile (52-sq-km) stretch of land along the eastern shore of Lake Tanganyika, by boat in July 1960. Goodall was eager to begin observing chimpanzees, but it wasn't as easy as she had hoped. The chimpanzees ran away whenever she got near. After approximately two months, Goodall's

It took months for Goodall to earn the trust of the chimpanzees she was studying.

21

luck changed. One day while she was sitting on the mountainside, she saw chimpanzees eating figs. She returned to the same spot every morning to watch. Goodall was slowly learning more about the chimpanzees each day.

A Different Kind of Scientist

Goodall was not a trained scientist. Instead she came up with her own ways to study chimpanzees. Unlike trained scientists, she didn't bring along books or other work to keep herself busy. Instead she spent entire days sitting still and watching. Sometimes she even slept in the bush at night so that she could stay near them. Most remarkably of all, Goodall named the chimpanzees she studied at a time when other scientists gave wild animals numbers. Numbering animals gave a scientist emotional distance from the animals being studied. But Goodall didn't want distance from the chimpanzees. She wanted the chimpanzee community to accept her as a friendly observer.

Goodall paid attention to the chimpanzee family relationships. She saw the strong bonds chimpanzee mothers had with their children and the way older chimpanzees played with their younger siblings. Goodall was learning about chimpanzee behavior. She observed that the chimpanzees were showing family relationships that were similar to human family relationships.

An Important Discovery

About a month after Goodall first saw the chimpanzees eating all kinds of fruits and leaves, such as figs, she saw something that

Flo the Chimp

Goodall named one chimpanzee Flo. Flo had at least five children: Faben, Figan, Fifi, Flint, and Flame, which Goodall also named. By watching Flo and her children, Goodall learned about chimpanzee families. Flo played with her children, chasing and tickling them. She let them play and explore, but she kept a close watch over them. She rushed to help them if they got into trouble. Goodall said that she learned a lot about how to be a good mother to her own child by watching Flo.

After only three months at Gombe, Goodall observed a chimpanzee using a stem as a tool.

changed the way people thought about chimpanzees and humans. A chimpanzee she had named David Greybeard used a straw-like stem to collect termites. He inserted the stem into the hole of a termite mound. He waited for a moment while termites grabbed hold of the stem. When he pulled the stem out of the hole, the termites hung on, and he ate the termites off the stem. Goodall watched David Greybeard repeat this many times.

In 1960 scientists believed that humans were the only animals that used tools. They believed that the ability to use tools was what made humans different from all of the other animals. Goodall's observation suddenly made her and Gombe the talk of scientists all around the world.

Goodall's Observations

After approximately five months, Goodall's mother returned to England. Goodall had shown that she was able to live safely at Gombe, so she was given permission to stay. She spent a lot of time alone with the chimpanzees. David Greybeard became Goodall's first chimpanzee friend. One day they sat near a stream. Goodall picked up a banana and offered it to him. He took the fruit from Goodall's hand and then held her hand. The friendship between Goodall and David Greybeard opened the path of acceptance for Goodall with the other chimpanzees. They no longer ran away when they saw her.

When Goodall began her study, scientists believed chimpanzees were herbivores, like gorillas, surviving mostly on fruits. Understanding how to find prey, working together to hunt, and using tools to kill and eat food were thought to be activities only humans could do. But Goodall witnessed these behaviors as chimpanzees ate pigs and monkeys, forcing scientists to think about how similar humans and chimpanzees are.

Goodall's Proudest Moment

During Goodall's first months at Gombe, the chimpanzees ran away from her. Then one day, David Greybeard and another chimpanzee let her sit so close to them that she could hear them breathing. Goodall said, "Without any doubt whatsoever, this was the proudest moment I had known. I had been accepted by the two magnificent creatures grooming each other in front of me."

Goodall Finally Goes to College

Goodall continued her work in Gombe through the 1960s. But she also left Africa for long periods of time to pursue a college education. Through the early 1960s, she spent half of each year at the University of Cambridge, earning a degree, and the other half of each year at Gombe.

Beginning in 1962, Goodall attended scientific conferences where she discussed her work with chimpanzees. Goodall was becoming a well-known scientist. Later that year, the National Geographic Society wanted to publish an article about her. The National Geographic Society's goal is to educate people about nature and science. The photographer they sent was Hugo van Lawick. During the time he lived at Gombe, van Lawick and Goodall fell in love. A year later, in 1963, the article about Goodall was published in *National Geographic* magazine, and Goodall became a celebrity.

In 1964 Goodall and van Lawick married. For the next two years, Goodall and van Lawick built a permanent research center at Gombe. It was a busy time for Goodall. She had her work at Gombe and college at Cambridge. She was also asked to attend scientific conferences. In 1966 Goodall earned her college degree. The next year, her son, Hugo Eric Louis van Lawick, was born.

Goodall, van Lawick, and their son, whom they called Grub, spent most of their time in Gombe and other parts of Africa.

Kind versus Cruel

Beginning in 1972, students from Stanford University in California came to Gombe for research. Around this time, Goodall's view of chimpanzees changed. Goodall and her students observed a war between two groups of chimpanzees as they fought over territory. They saw an adult female chimpanzee kill the infant of another female chimpanzee and then eat it. They also saw gangs of male chimpanzees attack lone chimpanzees from the other group. Goodall observed that, like humans, chimpanzees could be brutal and cruel.

While observing the war between the chimpanzee groups, Goodall began to think about how the chimpanzee gangs treated their victims the same way they treated prey animals, or animals they hunted for food. She called this being "de-chimpized."

Goodall thought about how this cruelty exists in both chimpanzees and humans. But she also remembered the compassion chimpanzees show each other. She wanted to learn how chimpanzees and humans could choose to be kind and compassionate instead of cruel. If chimpanzees could choose to be kind, Goodall thought, then so could humans.

CHAPTER FOUR

CHIMPANZEE ACTIVIST

n 1986 Goodall and other chimpanzee experts met at a conference in Chicago, Illinois. Goodall and other researchers considered what might be the cause of the rapidly-shrinking numbers of chimpanzees. Chimpanzees had been an endangered species since 1975. In 1900 there were 2 million wild chimpanzees living in Africa. By 1986 there were only 150,000.

Goodall speaks around the world, sharing her knowledge on chimpanzees and encouraging activism.

Chimpanzees at Risk

Goodall and many others wondered what was causing the number of wild chimpanzees to shrink. They could find only one answer, and it was disturbing.

People were the cause. Humans cut down forests where chimpanzees lived. Chimpanzees caught diseases from humans. Humans hunted chimpanzees for food. Female chimpanzees were killed. Their babies were stolen and sold to zoos or science labs.

Fighting Deforestation

Goodall learned that the people living close to chimpanzees in Africa were cutting down forest trees for lumber and firewood. They sold the lumber to buy food for their families or used it to build fires to cook their food. But this deforestation was destroying wild chimpanzees' habitats. Goodall thought that if people in Africa could grow their own farms to feed themselves, they would not have to cut down forests to sell the lumber and they could better provide for themselves. Goodall's goal is to teach people, especially young people, that humans are connected to all life on Earth.

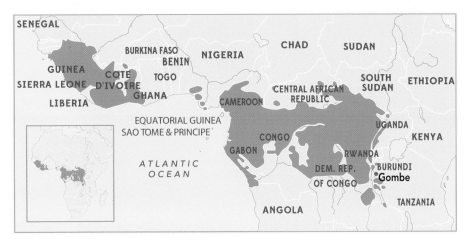

Chimpanzees in the Wild

This map of Africa shows where wild chimpanzees live today. In 1900 there were approximately 2 million wild chimpanzees. Today there are between 150,000 and 300,000 wild chimpanzees. How does this map help you visualize the population of chimpanzees in the wild? Find an earlier map of chimpanzee habitats and their populations. How does this map differ? How is it similar?

Goodall was upset by what she learned at the conference. From that point on, the focus of her work changed. Instead of observing chimpanzees, Goodall became a chimpanzee activist, working to improve the lives of chimpanzees. Goodall realized that to do this she needed to learn as much as she could about the people who were harming chimpanzees. She visited zoos and science labs to see for herself how chimpanzees lived in captivity. Then she made a plan.

Goodall believes teaching children about chimpanzees will encourage them to support conservation efforts.

Chimpanzee Conservation

Goodall realized that many of the people harming chimpanzees didn't know that chimpanzees are intelligent animals and are very similar to humans. So Goodall visited schools to teach students about chimpanzees, hoping that the students would make kind choices as they grew up. She met with government officials, urging them to write laws to protect chimpanzees. She also worked to fight deforestation, which was taking away the chimpanzees' habitats.

Goodall had founded the Jane Goodall Institute in 1977 to help fund her chimpanzee research at Gombe. After the 1986 conference, though, Goodall realized that saving and protecting wild chimpanzees was just as important as researching them. The Jane Goodall Institute held fundraisers to set up chimpanzee sanctuaries—safe homes for sick, injured, or orphaned chimpanzees.

FURTHER EVIDENCE

There is quite a bit of information about how chimpanzees have become endangered in Chapter Four. This chapter also explains how Goodall works to protect chimpanzees. What is the main point of this chapter? What key evidence supports this point? Read the article about chimpanzee conservation at the website below. Find a quote from the website that supports the chapter's main point. Does the quote support an existing piece of evidence in the chapter? Does it add a new one?

Jane Goodall Institute
mycorelibrary.com/jane-goodall

CHAPTER FIVE

VOICE OF PEACE

Since the 1990s, Goodall's work with chimpanzees has been focused on protecting them. She has written many books and articles about chimpanzees that have helped educate people all around the world. As a result, there is more awareness about the need to save chimpanzees.

In 2003 Queen Elizabeth II honored Goodall with the title of Dame of the British Empire.

In 1991 a group of 12 young people met with Goodall to discuss the problems they saw in their communities and in the world. This meeting was the beginning of Goodall's Roots & Shoots program. The goal of the program is to encourage young people to take action in making their own communities better places. Since 1991 Roots & Shoots has grown to more than 150,000 members in 130 countries.

In 2002 Goodall was named a United Nations Messenger of Peace for her "dedication to what is best in mankind." As

Roots & Shoots

Goodall's Roots & Shoots program teaches children to look at their own communities and neighborhoods to see what change is needed. From there, the groups work together to create a project to help. The project includes compiling a list of all the problems and writing a plan to solve those problems. Roots & Shoots projects help people, animals, and the environment. According to Goodall, "The most important message of Roots & Shoots is that every single individual makes a difference. Every individual has a role to play. Every one of us impacts the world around us everyday."

a Messenger of Peace, Goodall talks to children and adults around the world about how to bring peace to their communities.

Hope for the Future

Today Goodall is a popular speaker all around the world. She spends roughly 300 days each year traveling and speaking. In her talks, Goodall reminds her listeners that there are many reasons to have hope for the future. People are intelligent and don't give up easily, and these qualities will help them solve the problems facing humankind today.

Goodall turned 80 years old in 2014. She has taught the world that chimpanzees are not so different from humans,

TCRC

In 1992 the Jane Goodall Institute set up the Tchimpounga Chimpanzee Rehabilitation Center (TCRC) in the Republic of the Congo in Africa. The TCRC serves as a safe home for orphaned chimpanzees. It is set up to be as similar to the wild as possible. Chimpanzees at the TCRC have room to roam and are able to bond with each other.

Throughout her life, Goodall has made important scientific discoveries that have changed the way we think about chimpanzees and ourselves.

that chimpanzees and all living things deserve to be treated with respect, and that it is up to humans to save and protect all life on Earth. According to Goodall, the most important lesson of all is to work toward peace with compassion and love.

In 2002 Goodall gave a speech about the importance of teaching people about nonviolence so that they will make the world safer for all living things:

> The philosophy is very simple. We do not believe in violence. No violence. No bombs. That's not the way to solve problems. Violence leads to violence, at least in my view. So . . . the tools to solve the problems are knowledge and understanding: Know the facts, but see how they fit in the big picture. Hard work and persistence—don't give up—and love and compassion leading to respect for all life.

Source: Jane Goodall. "What Separates Us from Chimpanzees?" TED. TED Conferences, March 2002. Web. Accessed October 8, 2014.

Consider Your Audience

Review this passage closely. Consider how you would adapt it for a different audience, such as your parents, your classmates, or younger children. Write a blog post conveying this same information for the new audience. How does your new approach differ from the original text and why?

What We Know about Chimpanzees

When Goodall observed David Greybeard using stems to fish for termites, she knew that she had made an important discovery. Until that time, scientists classified humans as the only species capable of crafting tools. Because of Goodall's observations, scientists now know that humans aren't the only animals to make and use tools.

Omnivores Like Us

Scientists now know that chimpanzees are omnivores. Before Goodall arrived at Gombe, scientists believed that chimpanzees had a diet similar to gorillas. Scientists thought that chimpanzees were herbivores. But not long after observing David Greybeard fish for termites, Goodall saw him eating a small antelope. During her research, Goodall observed chimpanzees form groups to hunt small mammals, such as pigs and monkeys. She saw how they worked together to succeed.

Chimpanzee Relationships

Goodall's observations of Flo and her children changed the way humans thought about chimpanzee families. Goodall observed older brothers and sisters taking care of their younger siblings. She observed how close chimpanzee children were to their mothers and how depressed they became when their mothers died. This discovery has shown how similar chimpanzee behavior is to human behavior.

STOP AND THINK

Surprise Me

Chapter Three discusses wild chimpanzee behavior. After reading this book, what two or three facts about wild chimpanzees did you find most surprising? Write a few sentences about each fact. Why did you find each fact surprising?

Tell the Tale

Chapter One discusses Goodall's childhood. Describe the sights and sounds. What does she see? What might she be worried about as the world enters World War II? Be sure to set the scene, develop a sequence of events, and write a conclusion.

Why Do I Care?

Chimpanzees and humans are different species. But that doesn't mean you can't find similarities between your life and the world of wild chimpanzees. What do you have in common with wild chimpanzees? Use your imagination!

You Are There

This book discusses what Gombe was like when Jane Goodall first arrived. Imagine you are with Goodall at Gombe in 1960. How does living in the bush make you feel? What kinds of animals do you see?

GLOSSARY

activist
a person who works or
demonstrates for political
causes

omnivore
an animal that eats both
plants and animals

anthropologist
a scientist who studies
humans

paleontologist
a scientist who studies fossils

evolution
the process by which plants
and animals change over time

prehistoric
existing in times before
written history

fossil
the remains of a plant or
animal preserved in earth
or rock

LEARN MORE

Books

Silvey, Anita. *Untamed: The Wild Life of Jane Goodall.* Washington, DC: National Geographic, 2015.

Winter, Jeanette. *The Watcher: Jane Goodall's Life with the Chimps.* New York: Schwartz & Wade, 2011.

Websites

To learn more about Great Minds of Science, visit **booklinks.abdopublishing.com**. These links are routinely monitored and updated to provide the most current information available.

Visit **mycorelibrary.com** for free additional tools for teachers and students.

INDEX

ABOUT THE AUTHOR

Lois Sepahban lives with her husband and two children on a small farm in Kentucky. She has written several nonfiction books for children.